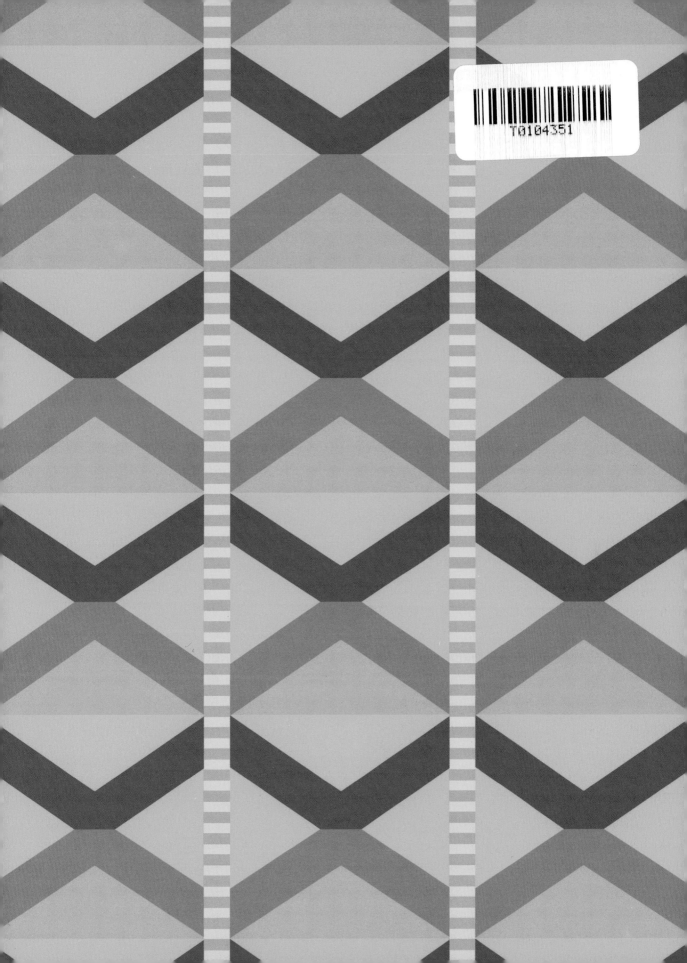

FAITH RINGGOLD

Narrating the world in pattern and color

Written by
Sharna Jackson

Illustrated by
Andrea Pippins

Faith Willie Jones was born, screaming, in Harlem
Hospital in New York City on October 8, 1930.

She was welcomed by her mother, Willie—
a dressmaker and designer—and her father, "Big"
Andrew—a bold, bright man who drove a truck.

Faith was known as The Baby,
even when she wasn't one anymore.

She was the youngest. First, there was "Little" Andrew, who was six when Faith was born. Her sister, Barbara, was three. Faith had another brother, Ralph. He sadly died of pneumonia at just 16 months old, before Faith was born.

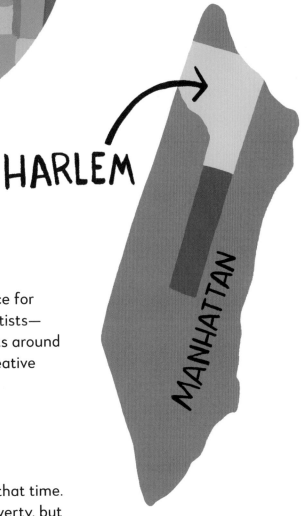

HARLEM

MANHATTAN

Harlem was a very important place for Black people—especially Black artists— when Faith was a child. The streets around her apartment were filled with creative people who would visit, talk, and practice music.

It wasn't all fun, though.

America was especially tough at that time. There was racism, sexism, and poverty, but Faith was always protected by her family.

Faith's apartment was busy. Guests would stay for dinner having fun, fascinating conversations with her father.

What sort of stories do you like? Funny ones? Scary ones?

At seven o'clock, the children would go to bed—even if they weren't tired. They would lie awake and listen to the adults talk about their dreams, dramas, and the daily news.

Sometimes, Little Andrew would whisper scary stories and Faith would squeal and shudder under her bed cover.

Faith spent a lot of time there, in bed. She developed asthma, and while she recuperated, Faith spun her own stories.

She began imagining worlds and the people who lived in them.

Faith's father bought her her first easel,
and she turned to art to share her stories.
In bed, propped up on her pillows, Faith
would draw and color while her mother
cooked, cleaned, and sewed around her.

Sometimes, Faith and her mother would visit theaters across New York, seeing stage shows in the afternoons. There, she saw amazing musicians like Cab Calloway, Louis Armstrong, Frank Sinatra, Billie Holiday, and Ella Fitzgerald.

What's your favorite song? Why?

When she was well enough for school,
Faith quickly became the class artist.
She created chalk drawings on the blackboard
and painted murals on thick paper.

Faith continued to create as a teenager and decided to go to art college in 1950. She had vivid memories of watching students travel there, walking up the hill from the subway, and she dreamed she would go there, too.

But the college accepted only men.

Undeterred, Faith went to the School of Education, part of City College, and studied art there instead, to become an art teacher.

One of Faith's first assignments was to design a playing card. She created a jack of diamonds in red, yellow, blue, and purple paint.

Faith spent her spare time trying new materials and techniques, such as using airbrushes and oil paints. To fully focus, Faith got her first studio space.

Have you ever tried drawing a family member or a friend?

In November 1950, Faith married Robert "Earl" Wallace, a jazz pianist. They had two children in 1952—Michelle in January and Barbara in December. Faith and Earl divorced in 1954.

Faith often painted portraits of her daughters when they were asleep. She was searching for her own images to paint—something she had not learned in school.

Faith graduated from City College in June 1955.

Faith had an excellent education, but she didn't yet know much about African or African American art. This troubled her.

She began to teach children art in 1955 and spent summers in Massachusetts painting everything she could see around her—boats, the ocean, houses, and landscapes.

Faith took her first trip to Europe with her mother and daughters in 1961.

The family sailed across the Atlantic aboard the luxurious ocean liner *SS Liberté* on its last voyage, enjoying delicious French-food feasts.

If you could go on vacation anywhere in the world, where would you go and what would you draw?

On land, they saw the *Mona Lisa* in the Louvre in Paris. They traveled to Nice by train, where they spent mornings and evenings on the beach. In Florence, they went to the Uffizi to see famous paintings. There, they were followed by curious monks who had never seen African American people before.

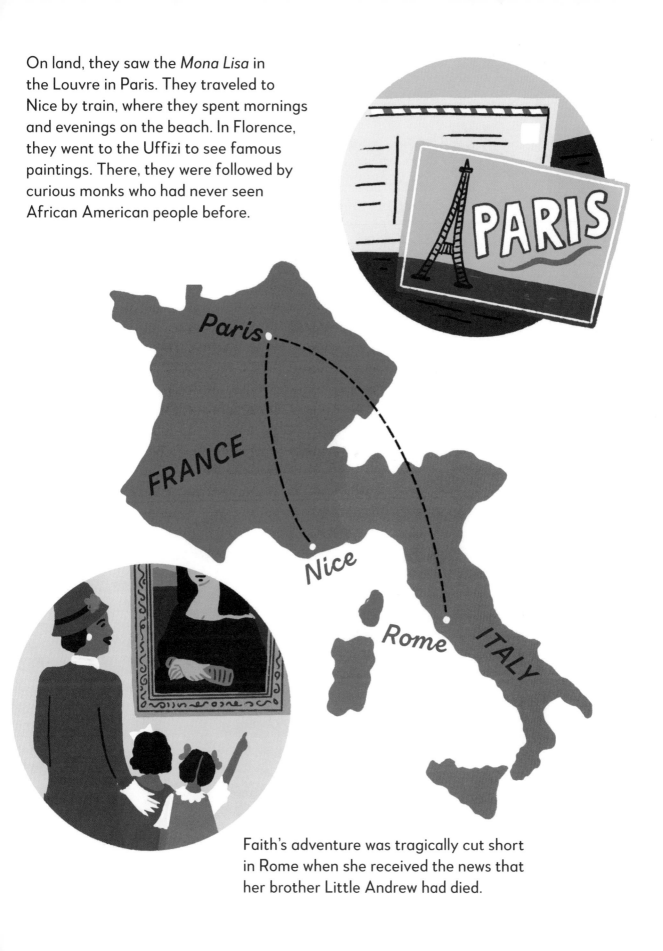

Faith's adventure was tragically cut short in Rome when she received the news that her brother Little Andrew had died.

Back in New York, Faith decided to find a gallery to look after her work. This was a difficult task for Black artists in the 1960s. Most galleries had white owners who weren't interested in Black artists' work.

Faith and Burdette "Birdie" Ringgold—her second husband, whom she married in 1962—would carry armfuls of her work to the many galleries in Manhattan, only to be turned away.

One day, Faith and Birdie showed a gallery owner
her paintings of beautiful landscapes and flowers.

The owner said, "*You* can't do *this*."

Faith and Birdie talked about this on their way home.

Radical changes were happening across the world.
Faith realized she needed to paint more than
pretty plants. She needed to tell her story.

That meeting changed Faith's work forever.

From this point on, Faith's work became political.
She was inspired by events that she saw in the present—
and from her past—and her art reflected this.

Her *American People* Series began in 1963 during the
Civil Rights Movement—a time when Black people
and their allies struggled to obtain equal rights.

One of the first paintings, *#2 For Members Only*, focused on an incident of racism Faith experienced on a church outing. A gang of white men gathered around her group with sticks and told them to get back on their bus.

In 1967, Faith's *#20 Die* concluded the series. It is a huge mural that shows the violence of the riots as people fought for their freedom. Faith had been caught in the confusion of a number of riots. She saw blood on the streets and people running to rescue their children from the chaos.

Faith was political in her studio and on the street, too.

She was part of many anti-racist and feminist groups. She was once arrested after protesting at a major museum of American art for two years, because their exhibitions severely lacked diversity.

As part of these protests, Faith and her friends would leave rotten eggs in the museum. They would stand on the museum steps and blow whistles to confuse the guards.

Faith also worked with women who were held at the Women's House of Detention on Rikers Island. She interviewed the prisoners there to understand what they would like to see in a work of art.

Their ideas were incorporated into a mural called
For The Women's House (1971), which shows women in
roles that were at that time mostly occupied by men:
basketball players, bus drivers, and police officers.

During the 1970s, Faith explored many different materials
and began making masks and soft hanging sculptures.
These were based on both real and imagined people.
She would create her masks from linen she painted.
Then she would add beads and weave
in parts of palm trees for hair.

Try making your own masks,
as Faith did.

Brushes

Palm leaves

Fabric

Beads

Paint

Together with her mother, who was a talented designer, they created
the *Witch Mask Series*—11 works inspired by African traditions.

It was important to Faith that the masks were worn and not
just displayed. She added costumes to the masks, which made
them perfect for performance. Those performances
included storytelling, music, and dance.

Faith went to West Africa twice in the 1970s.

She had been desperate to visit since the 1960s, so she could see the fabrics, masks, and sculptures from Ghana and Nigeria that had been inspiring her. She wanted to investigate her roots.

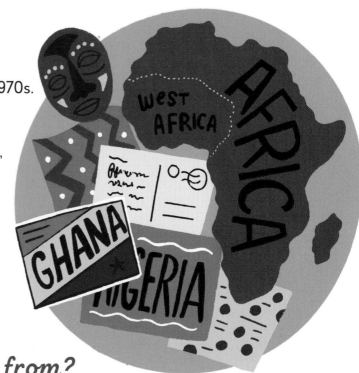

Where are your ancestors from? Have you been there?

In 1977, she represented America—along with 250 other artists—for the Second World Black and African Festival of Arts and Culture held in Lagos, in Nigeria.

During the opening ceremony, Faith and her fellow Americans circled the stadium to tremendous cheer. They sang and made the Black Power salute, with each section of the stadium shouting "Black Power!" in return.

Using brocade fabric she bought in a market in Lagos, Faith began making bolder masks, with many more beads, feathers, and details.

Faith's experiences traveling, working in new ways, and wanting to move away from painting led her to quilting—an art form that Faith is now famous for.

Quilting, sewing, and weaving are tied to women, working in the home, and African traditions. As a child, Faith fondly remembered her mother designing dresses and teaching her to sew. Her mother would give her scraps of fabric and she would try to make shoes and purses.

They worked together again in 1980 on Faith's first quilt, *Echoes of Harlem*. Faith painted a series of portraits for the middle of the work and surrounded them with a quilted border.

Their collaboration made the work extra special.

Faith wanted to share stories, and she wanted them to be read. She began including words on her quilts.

In 1985, she created the fictional *Street Story Quilt*, a tale she set in a building in Harlem. There are 15 windows in the building, and the story, set over many years, is written above them.

What's your **favorite way** to share stories? Who do you share them with?

There are three parts, each narrated by a character named Grace.
Grace is inspired by the storytellers Faith overheard as a child,
when she was sent to bed at seven o'clock, all those years ago.

In the first panel, *The Accident*, we learn about 10-year-old A.J.
who, with his grandmother, has witnessed a car accident.

The Fire, the second panel, depicts a blaze that ends with A.J.'s father's death.

The final panel, *The Homecoming*, shows A.J. all grown up and successful,
returning to the building to collect his grandmother.

Faith published her first children's book in 1991. *Tar Beach* is based on a quilt created in 1988 and also her childhood.

On hot summer nights, Faith, her family, and friends would visit their Tar Beach—the asphalt roof of her building in Harlem. They would take blankets, sandwiches, and lemonade. The children would snack and look at the stars, while the adults talked and played cards. They could see as far as the George Washington Bridge.

In her book, the narrator Cassie visits her own tar beach. There, she thinks about her life and dreams she can fly over buildings, taking them over to improve her family's life.

In all of her books, Faith blends reality and fantasy to deal with issues around racism optimistically.

Why not write a short story that turns your ordinary day into an extraordinary one!

There was 28 of us and one newborn baby on that long hard sojourn through the woods and swamps, we named the baby Freedom because she was born almost free. By day we prayed for the black of night to cover us. By night we crept softly to muffle our steps.

3/40   Under a Blood Red Sky   faith Ringgold 2/5/01

The issues Faith saw in the 1960s are, unfortunately, still relevant today. Racism persists and protest remains powerful. Faith's work continues to resonate.

From 2000, Faith worked on a series of prints called *Under a Blood Red Sky*, which sometimes have an additional title—*Coming to Jones Road*.

Faith and Birdie left Harlem in 1992 for Jones Road in Englewood, New Jersey. Faith dreamed of a studio in the country, but not too far from Harlem. There, the couple faced a series of racist incidents from their neighbors.

Faith kept on going.

What Faith saw is now seen and loved by people across the world
in her art. She has been named in songs and on television programs,
and she even has a school named after her in California.

Faith doesn't struggle to find galleries now. She's seen her work
exhibited hundreds of times, including at solo exhibitions. Her first
European solo show was at the Serpentine in London in 2019.

Faith saw the classroom again, returning to teaching in 1987, retiring in 2002.

In her home, Faith sees a shelf full of books she's written, including her autobiography and 17 books created for children.

Faith still sees the country in Englewood and did so with Birdie, until he died in 2020.

Faith continues to work in her studio at home.

She keeps going.

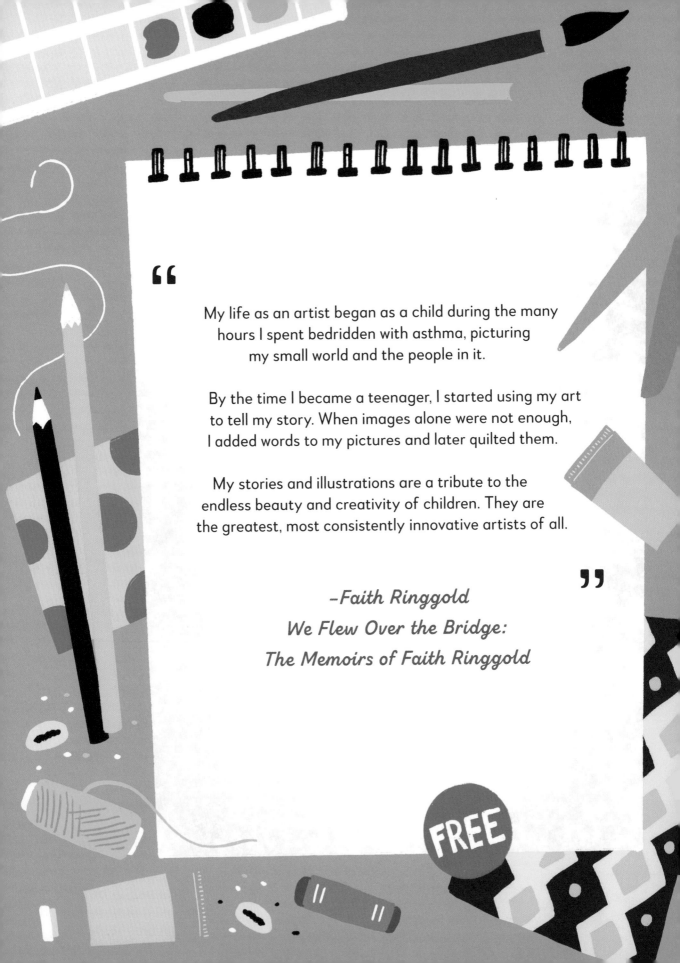

> My life as an artist began as a child during the many hours I spent bedridden with asthma, picturing my small world and the people in it.
>
> By the time I became a teenager, I started using my art to tell my story. When images alone were not enough, I added words to my pictures and later quilted them.
>
> My stories and illustrations are a tribute to the endless beauty and creativity of children. They are the greatest, most consistently innovative artists of all.

—Faith Ringgold
We Flew Over the Bridge:
The Memoirs of Faith Ringgold

FREE

Key artworks

Faith has produced art in many different materials, from fabric to painted canvas. These pieces are filled with considered, minute detail and often combine words with pictures, interweaving the stories she wished to tell. Take a closer look at these pieces, all in the collection of The Metropolitan Musem of Art, New York City.

What do you like most about Faith's artworks?

1985 *Street Story Quilt*

Cotton canvas, acrylic paint, ink marker, dyed and printed cotton, and sequins, sewn to a cotton flannel backing

Key artworks continued:

1990   *Freedom of Speech*
Acrylic and graphite
on paper

2001

Under a Blood Red Sky
Colored etching

There was 28 of us and one newborn baby on that long hard sojourn through the woods and swamps, we named the baby Freedom because she was born almost free. By day we prayed for the black of night to cover us. By night we crept softly to muffle our steps.

3/40   Under a Blood Red Sky   faith Ringgold 2/5/01

Uncle Tate could vanish in a flash and turn up in the same time and place at the same time and way, One day they just up an walk to freedom nobody could be in two places

Aunt Emmy

Coming to Jones Road: Under a Blood Red Sky #8   faith Ringgold 2007

2007

Coming to Jones Road Under a Blood Red Sky #8, from *Femfolio*
Digital print with hand lithography

The art of observation

Faith knows our world is full of surprises—sometimes you just have to look closely. She has spent her life looking for and listening to stories to inspire her in her work, then adding a little bit of magic to her reality.

Try this observation challenge yourself. Get some paper and pens and grab a clock, a watch, or a phone. Check the time—you'll need 20 minutes for the first stage.

What can you see?

Look out of a window, any window—it could be at home, at school, or at your friend's house. Sit outside if the weather is nice.

Sketch the scene in front of you or make notes on what you see— and what you don't see.

Feel free to add some fiction! What buildings are in view? Did you see any people? Where do you think they're going next? What might they be having for dinner? Can they fly?!

After 20 minutes, stop looking. Then, later, use your notes and ideas to create a six-panel comic strip on what you saw and what you thought or imagined.

The art of activism

Faith is passionate about making the world a fairer place. Some of her work is political, and she took part in many protests. What's important to you? What would you like to change in the world? Be inspired by Faith to make a change.

Try this yourself!

Choose a cause and take action: It could be a big topic like racism, sexism, or homelessness, or it could be something smaller—the amount of trash in your local park, for example, or unhealthy school lunches.

WHAT CAUSE ARE YOU PASSIONATE ABOUT?

Think about **where** the problem is, **why** it's wrong and must change, and **what** you would like to see instead.

Figure out **how** you're going to communicate your concerns. You could write a letter, make a video, or create a poster.

Find out **who** you need to send your work to—and do just that!

Glossary

activism (*noun*)
Activities or actions that are created
to make changes in our world.

collaboration (*noun*)
Working with other people on a shared project.

fantasy (*noun*)
Something that is imaginary and not real; made up.

feminism (*noun*)
A movement working to make sure women
have the same rights as men.

mural (*noun*)
A large work of art often painted directly on a wall.

narrative (*noun*)
Events that happen in a story; the plot.

performance (*noun*)
Art made with music, acting, dance, and often puppets.

quilting (*noun*)
An art, craft, and leisure activity where pieces of fabric
are stitched together to make a larger work.

reality (*noun*)
Something that exists in our world; is not imagined.

Sharna Jackson

Sharna Jackson is an award-winning author and curator who specializes in developing and delivering socially engaged initiatives for children and young people across culture, publishing, and entertainment. She was the Artistic Director at Site Gallery, an international contemporary art space in Sheffield, UK, and was the editor of the BAFTA-nominated Tate Kids website. Sharna's debut novel *High-Rise Mystery* has received numerous awards and accolades, including the Waterstones Book Prize for the Best Book for Younger Readers 2020 and the *Sunday Times* Book of the Week. Sharna's activity books for Tate won the FILAF award for Best Children's Art Book in 2015. Sharna lives on a ship in Rotterdam in the Netherlands.

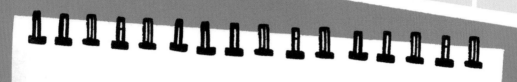

Andrea Pippins

Andrea Pippins is an illustrator and author who has a passion for creating images that reflect what she wants to see in art, media, and design. Some of her previous works include *Who Will You Be*, *Becoming Me*, and *I Love My Hair*. In her artwork Andrea enjoys using vibrant color and bold patterns, and celebratory details to tell her visual stories. Andrea lives in Stockholm, Sweden, where you can often find her dancing in her living room with samba music all the way up.
Learn more at andreapippins.com.

Senior Editor Emma Grange
Senior Designer Anna Formanek
Project Editor Rosie Peet
Designer Clare Baggaley
Picture Researchers Martin Copeland and Taiyaba Khatoon
Production Editor Siu Yin Chan
Senior Production Controller Louise Minihane
Senior Acquisitions Editor Katy Flint
Managing Editor Paula Regan
Managing Art Editors Jo Connor and Vicky Short
Publishing Director Mark Searle

First American Edition, 2021
Published in the United States by DK Publishing
1450 Broadway, Suite 801, New York, NY 10018

**The Metropolitan
Museum of Art**
New York

A catalog record for this book
is available from the Library of Congress.
ISBN 978-0-7440-3977-1

DK books are available at special discounts when purchased in bulk for sales
promotions, premiums, fund-raising, or educational use. For details, contact:
DK Publishing Special Markets,
1450 Broadway, Suite 801, New York, NY 10018
SpecialSales@dk.com

Printed and bound in China

Acknowledgments
DK would like to thank Sheena Wagstaff, Lisa Silverman Meyers,
Laura Barth, Leanne Graeff, Emily Blumenthal, and Morgan Pearce
at The Met; Hilary Becker; Clare Baggaley; Jennette ElNaggar at DK;
Sharna Jackson and Andrea Pippins; and above all Faith Ringgold,
Dorian Bergen, and Grace Matthews.

For the curious

www.dk.com
www.metmuseum.org

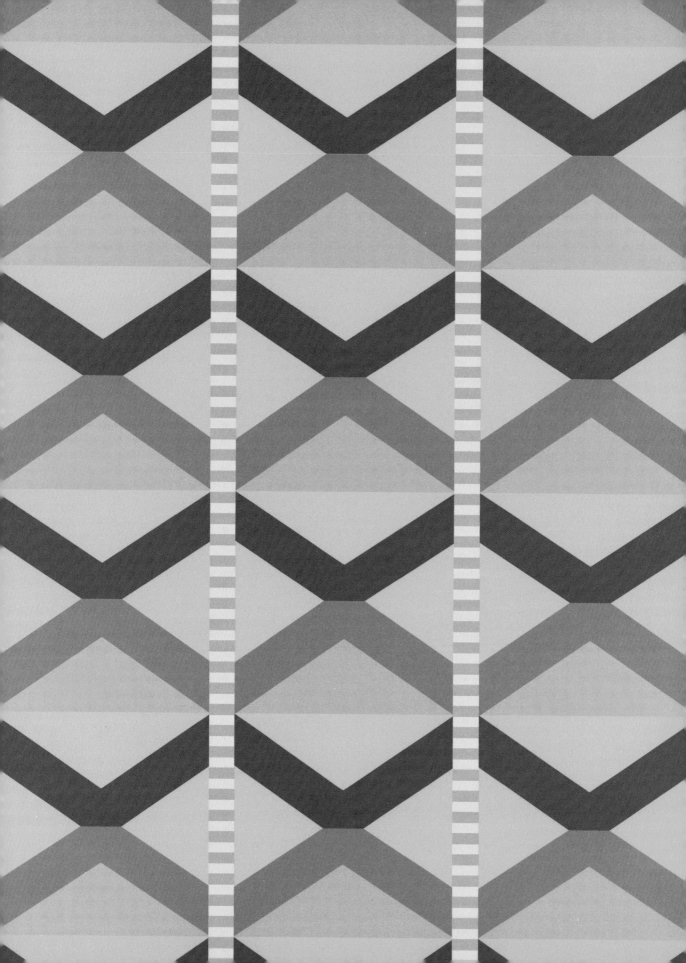